# MARIJUANA

A marijuana joint seems harmless, but it can damage your mind.

# MARIJUANA

Sandra Lee Smith

THE ROSEN PUBLISHING GROUP, INC.
NEW YORK

To my mom, Bettelee, who taught me early
to respect and value my life.

*The people pictured in this book are only models; they in no way
practice or endorse the activities illustrated. Captions serve only to
explain the subjets of photographs and do not in any way imply a
connection between the real-life models and the staged situations.*

Published in 1991, 1993, 1995 by The Rosen Publishing Group, Inc.
29 East 21st Street, New York, NY 10010

**Revised Edition, 1995**

Manufactured in the United States of America.

**Library of Congress Cataloging-in-Publication Data**

Smith, Sandra Lee
    Marijuana / Sandra Lee Smith
    (The Drug Abuse Prevention Library)
    Includes bibliographical references and Index
    Summary: Examines the ways marijuana has been produced
    and used, and discusses the harmful effects of the drug on the
    mind and body
        ISBN 0-8239-2125-5
        1. Marijuana—Juvenile literature
        2. Marijuana—United States—Juvinile literature
        [1. Marijuana. 2. Drug abuse.] I. Title. II. Series.
        HV5882. M3S575 1991
        362.29'5—dc20

90-45105
CIP
AC

# Contents

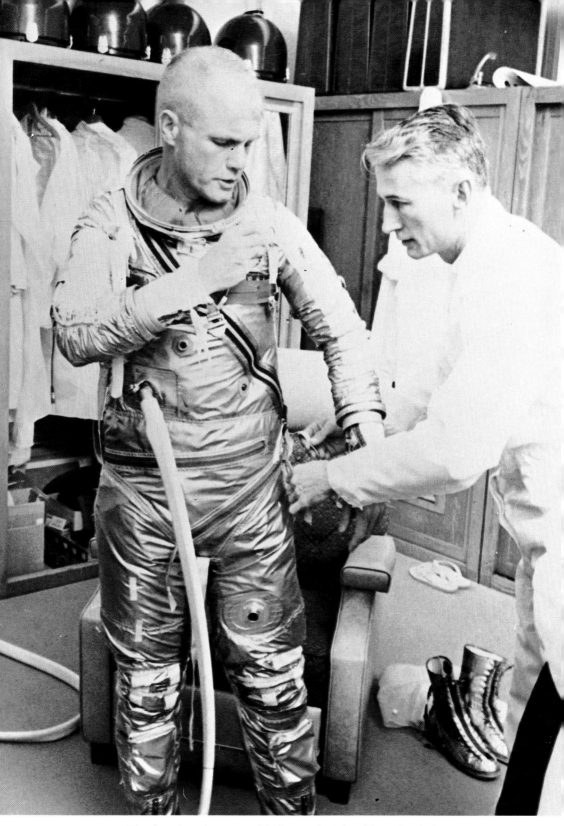

The first American to orbit the earth, John Glenn knew how important his space suit was to his life.

# Introduction

Marijuana is the most widely used illegal drug in America today. However, it is the least understood. Even doctors don't know all the facts about the effects of marijuana; everyday people know even less. There are thousands of myths about marijuana. Most of these myths were invented in order to make marijuana seem okay. However, like most myths, these are mostly wrong.

Understanding the myths about marijuana is important. You need to know the facts. The more you know about marijuana, the better prepared you'll be. This book will help you to learn the truth about the myths.

**8** ## Myth: Only a few people use marijuana.

Fact: Unfortunately, between 16 and 20 million people in America are frequent users, and almost half of all Americans have tried pot at least once.

## Myth: Marijuana is safe.

Fact: Smoking one marijuana cigarette, or *joint*, is as harmful to your lungs as smoking a pack of cigarettes. Frequent users often get bronchitis and other infections of the lungs. Marijuana kills brain cells, which causes the user to have memory problems. Brain cells, unlike other cells, do not grow back; all damage caused by marijuana is permanent.

For a pregnant woman, marijuana is especially dangerous. Not only does it affect the mother, it affects the fetus as well. Babies born to marijuana smokers are usually born smaller and may have distorted features.

Frequent marijuana use has many psychological effects as well. Users may lose interest in life and become lazy. Often people who smoke pot find it difficult to concentrate on anything more than television. Users may not be able to hold down a job or concentrate in school.

## Myth: Marijuana increases creativity.

Fact: Marijuana does not increase creativity. In fact, it can decrease it, as users become more and more lazy.

*State-dependent learning* is a psychological term meaning that if you learn to do something in one condition, you will always do that thing in the same state. For instance, if you read before bed every night, eventually you might have trouble going to sleep without reading. Many marijuana users believe that marijuana increases their creativity because they usually try to be creative while stoned. A person might smoke pot and paint a picture, and then decide that he can paint only while stoned. That's not true. He has simply trained his mind to think of painting while he's stoned. His mind learned to think of painting only while not sober.

## Myth: Marijuana is not addictive.

Fact: Marijuana is not considered physically addictive, but it might as well be. Pot is extremely addictive psychologically. Frequent smokers feel that they can't can't function without the aid of the drug. Sometimes people need the support of a recovery program to quit.

The marijuana plant grows wild all over the world.

# CHAPTER 1

# The Usage and History of Marijuana

The scientific name for the marijuana plant is *Cannabis sativa*. Marijuana is actually the Spanish word; the word for the plant in English is *hemp*. It has many slang names, among them "grass," "pot," "weed," "ganja," "herb," and "Mary Jane." Being high on marijuana also has many different slang names, such as "stoned," "baked," "fried," and "zooted."

Marijuana is a tall, strong-smelling plant. It is extremely strong and can grow just about anywhere. Hemp has been used for centuries to make paper, rope, and clothing because of its strength and because it is so easy to find and grow. Rope made of hemp is very strong.

The amounts of the chemicals in marijuana plants change enormously. They are different depending on where

*12* the plant grows, the time of year, even the time of day. That's why plants grown in Mexico have so many more chemicals than those grown in the US. That's also why there are different qualities of marijuana; depending on where the plant was grown, it will make you more or less high.

Marijuana contains more than 400 different chemicals. However, only one chemical is responsible for the high feeling. This chemical is called THC. The THC expands the blood vessels in the lungs and in the brain, letting more oxygen into the rest of the system. It lowers the blood pressure and speeds up the heart. Because of the lowered blood pressure, less blood flows into the brain. This is why you feel high, or light-headed. It's something like hyperventilating. Unfortunately, with frequent use the blood vessels can be damaged.

The most common form of marijuana sold is a mixture of leaves, seeds, and stems. The seeds and stems are removed, and the leaves are most often smoked in a joint, or "reefer" or "jay." The butts of joints, called "roaches," contain the most THC of the joint. These can be smoked using a "roach clip." Sometimes pot is smoked in other ways too. It can be smoked in a pipe. It can be smoked in a *bong*, a jar or plastic tube with water in the bottom to filter the smoke. Usually pipes and bongs are used with stronger marijuana to avoid burning the lungs.

Sometimes the resin is pressed out of the plant's leaves and hardened. The cake produced is called hashish, or hash. Such cakes are much stronger than the leaves alone. Distilled resin is called hash oil. This is the strongest form of marijuana. Often hash oil is put into food or drinks. Hash brownies, brownies made with hash oil, are a favorite food of users.

## History

Marijuana was known for its mind-altering properties as far back as 2737 BC. It was common in China and in India. It was not used as a drug in America for many years. It was called "ditch weed" because it could be found in just about any ditch in the country. The plant was mostly used for making cloth. Then, during World War I, Mexican migrant workers began bringing pot with them to the United States. Marijuana has been brought across the Mexican-American border ever since.

Owning marijuana was made a crime

The marijuana that grows in Mexico is much stronger than the American variety.

in 1937, when Congress passed the Marijuana Tax Act. The drug was still somewhat common, however, despite the law.

Then the 1960s hit. This was a time of civil protest, when many of the youths of the country were trying to change what they thought was the old-fashioned morality of America. These protests changed many outdated laws and opened the minds of many. However, many people involved in these protests smoked pot. Even less was known about the drug then, and even more people believed the myth that marijuana was not harmful. Many youths also felt that smoking pot made as much of a statement as marching in a protest.

At the same time, Americans were suffering through the Vietnam War. Many soldiers in Vietnam began doing drugs because they were easy to get, and they needed an escape. Many of these soldiers then brought their drug use home.

Since that time, marijuana use has been growing. American plants have been crossbred to create a new plant that has a THC level two to ten times higher than in foreign marijuana. Some of these types, nicknamed "skunk," contain 12 to 18 percent THC.

**16**     Until recently, marijuana was still legal if prescribed by a doctor. It was used with some success in the treatment of eye problems and the side effects of cancer treatments. However, the government decided that the harm done by marijuana outweighs its good effects, and now it is illegal to buy or sell pot for any reason.

Unfortunately, because of not-so-strict laws controlling marijuana, it is easy to get. The average age when most people start using pot is 13 in the United States. Marijuana is the second-largest cash crop. So whether you try it is up to you.

Most teenagers do not get their marijuana from criminals or gang members. Most get it from their friends. Very often one person brings pot to a party and shares it with everyone there. You may know someone who deals weed at your school. Marijuana is so common in the United States that you can almost forget that it's illegal. However, you can be arrested for having just one joint.

Many people purposely buy pot that is laced with other drugs. A joint laced with PCP ("angel dust") is called a "lovely," with cocaine a "primo," and with both, a "screamo." Sometimes you can get laced pot without knowing it.

Strong marijuana is smoked through water to keep it from burning the lungs.

**18**     Governments in all countries are trying to stop the marijuana trade. They spray fields of marijuana with *paraquat,* a weed-killer. However, the drug growers don't want to lose their harvest, so they often sell the marijuana even after it's been sprayed with poison. Many people who have smoked weed laced with poison have become very sick, or even died.

Sometimes, for no particular reason, people lace marijuana with poisons before they sell it. One kind of lace used is asthma medicine. For some people, this can cause extreme difficulty in breathing; those who smoke pot laced with asthma medicine have been known to faint, or even to fall into a coma.

There is no way to tell normal marijuana from laced marijuana. It looks the same; it smells the same. It's only after you start getting sick that you realize that what you smoked was laced.

A new form of laced marijuana has recently emerged: "illy." This is marijuana laced with *formaldehyde*. Formaldehyde is a chemical used to preserve dead bodies. Obviously, it is not very good for live ones. Illy almost always makes the smoker very sick.

Most teenagers do not smoke marijuana every day. They might smoke at parties, or in social situations. The name for this type of user is a *social user*. A hard-core user, or "stoner," however, uses every day. He cannot get through a day without it. Most addicts don't pay attention to what's going on around them; the world is too confusing. They cannot keep their minds focused on one thing, instead they mentally wander all over the place. They have very little memory and have trouble keeping themselves together.

Joints of marijuana are rolled in paper like cigarettes.

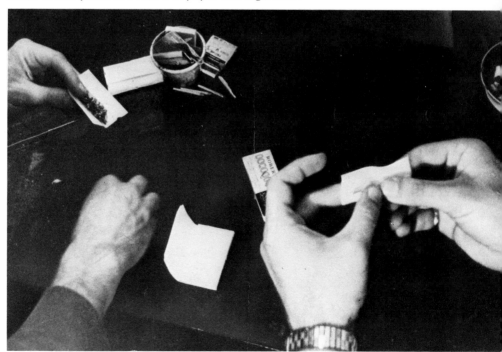

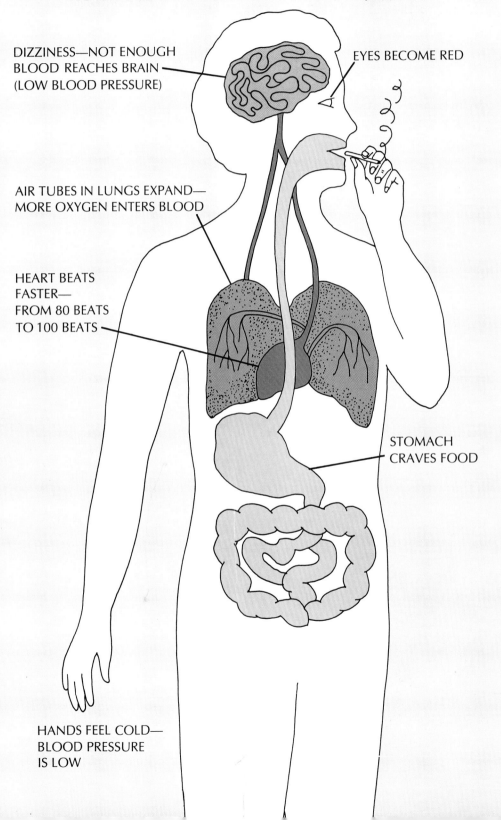

# HOW YOUR BODY IS AFFECTED BY MARIJUANA

DIZZINESS—NOT ENOUGH
BLOOD REACHES BRAIN
(LOW BLOOD PRESSURE)

EYES BECOME RED

AIR TUBES IN LUNGS EXPAND—
MORE OXYGEN ENTERS BLOOD

HEART BEATS
FASTER—
FROM 80 BEATS
TO 100 BEATS

STOMACH
CRAVES FOOD

HANDS FEEL COLD—
BLOOD PRESSURE
IS LOW

# CHAPTER 2

# What Marijuana Does to You

Marijuana is a mind-altering drug. It changes the chemistry of the body and slows the thinking process. Because of that, many people think it helps them to relax. They think it helps them to stay calm. It doesn't. The following is what it really does.

In the body, THC makes the heart beat faster. It may beat from 80 beats a minute to 150. The air tubes in the lungs relax and become larger. More oxygen enters the blood. This extra oxygen is what causes the "high."

Other blood vessels relax too. The vessels in the eyes become larger and receive more blood. That makes the eyes red.

*21*

**22** When the vessels in the rest of the body relax, the blood pressure goes down. This drop makes the hands and feet feel cold. The low blood pressure also causes dizziness because not enough blood is reaching the brain.

The THC in the brain causes changes in the user's senses. All of a sudden the user may feel extremely thirsty or hungry. The "munchies" hit, and the user wants to eat everything in sight. The drug also distorts the way things appear. Many people think it makes them see art or hear music better. In fact, it only changes the appearance.

Even though we can show that these effects are bad, many people still want to use the drug. That is because for a short time it does make them feel good. When it is smoked, the user can feel light-headed and silly for about an hour. When it is eaten the effect lasts for about four hours. Sometimes people want to feel that way. At parties and with friends they laugh and have what seems like a good time when they are high on drugs.

The problem is that after the silliness is over the drug makes the user feel sleepy. Some users feel that way from the start. People react differently to the drug. They may want more so that they can keep the high, or they may be depressed as they come down.

Often people who are stoned become exceedingly paranoid. They are certain that they are going to get arrested at any moment, that the police are watching them, that their parents know what's going on. Sometimes the insecurities of the user come to light, and the user is convinced that everyone is saying bad things about him or her.

The morning after getting high, many people experience something rather like a hang-over from alcohol. This is often called being "burnt." Burnt people experience all the disorientation and slow-thinking of being stoned, with none of the giggles. Sometimes this difficulty in clear thinking can last for a week or longer.

There are many reasons people would ignore all these nasty things about marijuana and smoke it. Here are just a few.

## Lack of Motivation

Miguel took a hit off the joint, and then passed it to Neil. Neil inhaled deeply, smiled at Miguel, and then blew the smoke in perfect rings above his head. "Wow, man, you're good at that," Miguel said admiringly.

"Yeah, well, you do anything long enough and you get good. I can roll a mean joint, too." Neil leaned back against the bleacher support. They were cutting afternoon classes, sitting under the bleachers and smoking pot.

"This one sure is fine. How long you been smoking?" Miguel was curious. He had been friends with Neil for a long time. Whenever he didn't feel like dealing with school, he knew he could find Neil under the bleachers smoking pot.

"I don't know. A few years, I guess."

"Man, how do you cope? I mean, I'm out here smoking now, but I get so tired afterwards. No way could I do homework or keep my job at the deli if I did this all the time."

"I don't really care about school, and I get this stuff from my brother. I just stick to what I'm good at." Neil took another drag and blew more smoke rings. He passed the joint to Miguel.

"But what about college? What kind of job can you get without a college degree? I want to be a vet. I know it's going to be tough, but I can do it. Actually, I should stop doing this now while I can." He gave the joint back to Neil without taking a

Cutting school to get high is a waste of your life.

26 drag. "So, what about you? What do you want to do?"

"Who cares? I'll probably drive a truck like my old man. He never finished high school, and he's doing all right. Besides, you don't learn anything at school anyway. What does geology have to do with making a living? Or buying this?" Neil finished off the last bit of the joint. He closed his eyes and lay back, not caring about anything but getting something to eat. He was starving.

Miguel got up and left his friend lying there. He knew how much he wanted to graduate and go to vet school someday. He also knew that he wouldn't get there by smoking pot.

Often school seems meaningless. Some of the things that are taught don't seem to have much to do with real life. For that reason many teenagers want to forget about school. They want to find something more exciting. Often drugs are their answer.

Drugs do not have to be the only answer. Many things can be fun. Most schools have clubs or after-school activities. Many groups outside of school offer hobbies and sports. Religious orders often provide programs for teenagers. Most city

and town governments offer projects for *27*
them. There is always something to interest you if you look hard enough.

Becoming involved in other things takes
away the *need* for drugs. Drugs seem to
offer escape from boredom. If people are
doing lots of things, they do not have time
to get bored. Remember Miguel. He was
so full of his plans to become a veterinar-
ian that he didn't have time to waste
getting stoned on drugs. Have you
thought about what you want to do when
you finish high school? It's never too early
to begin planning for the kind of life you
want to lead.

## *False Courage*

"Look, Charmella, there he is. The man of
your dreams just waiting for you," teased
Aimee. Rico was surrounded by the usual
bunch of girls. He seemed bored, though,
and looked around as if looking for someone in particular.

Charmella blushed. "It's not like he
can't have any girl in school. If I could
take a few drags, this would be so much
easier."

"Charmella, don't be stupid. You don't
need that. Just go talk to him. He's ador-
able, and besides, it looks like he could

Teens who are stoned on marijuana often risk their lives in foolish stunts.

care less about any of the girls after him now." Aimee pushed her toward Rico.

Charmella stumbled, then caught her balance and reluctantly walked in Rico's direction. He saw her and waved her over, disappointing the girls already around him. Charmella began to get nervous. Her palms were cold and clammy. She wondered how her hair looked. Man, she thought, I wish I had a joint. She knew she should have put on lipstick. "Hi, Rico. What's up?"

"Thought you'd never get here. Lunch is over soon, but do you want to go for a walk before class?" Rico was so sexy, thought Charmella. "Yeah, sure." But I've got a test next, she thought. I'll make it back in time.

They walked toward the park next to school. Rico grabbed Charmella's hand and said, "I'm glad you finally talked to me. I noticed you a while ago, but I didn't think you liked me. Why is your hand so cold? Am I making you nervous?" Charmella nodded, still a little shy. If only...

"Hey, you want to try something? It will take the edge off your nerves." Rico stopped and pulled a plastic bag with four

30 joints in it out of his pocket. "Pot does wonders for your nerves. Here." He gave her one.

"Thanks." You'll never know how much this means, she thought. They both lit up. Charmella took a deep drag, held it, and blew it out. That was much better. She took Rico's hand, and they continued walking. Half a mile later they were stoned and didn't care whether or not they made it back to class at all.

Many people think that marijuana will help them to relax. It does change the body and blood makeup so that it seems that the body is relaxing. In fact, it causes low blood pressure, and that causes more stress to the body. Because the senses are changed, the mind thinks it is relaxed. But it is not.

There are many safe ways to relax. The best part about them is that they do not cost any money. The library has many books about exercises that help you relax. Some health insurance plans that parents have through their work offer stress release programs such as biofeedback and meditation.

City parks and public groups offer other activities and classes that relieve stress.

Yoga, martial arts, judo, and karate are examples. Many religious groups offer classes in meditation and in learning how to relax. These are all healthful and safe ways to control stress.

## Emotional Pain

Things at home for Gabe had just gotten worse and worse. Nothing had been easy since his mother died a year before. He had been busy taking care of the house and of his father when he got really drunk. He always had to do something.

When he walked into the house after school he could tell that today was a bad day. His father was sitting watching TV with a stack of beer cans next to his chair. Gabe tried to sneak behind him up the stairs, but his father turned suddenly.

"And where do you think you're going, you lazy waste of space?"

Gabe didn't say anything. He knew that any word from him would provoke his father into violence. He would take his chances that silence wouldn't do the same thing.

"And where have you been, anyway? You'd better get some food together, you little nothing. I'm not going to wait around all day."

*32*    Gabe turned quickly into the kitchen, wondering what dinner would take the least time to make.

"Don't you walk away when I'm speaking to you!" Gabe's father shouted. Gabe felt the hand on his arm before he knew his father had gotten up. His father twisted him around to face him, and then shoved him backward. "You never show any respect. I'm going to teach you some manners if I have to break your neck!" He swung his fist at Gabe, but Gabe ducked and pulled away from his father. "Get back here!" his father yelled as Gabe ran out of the house.

Gabe just wandered around for a while. He couldn't go home until he was certain his dad was asleep, that was sure. He decided to go to the park. He could sit there and calm down for a while.

When Gabe got to the park, he saw a group of people from his school sitting around on the benches. He wasn't really close with any of them, but he had nothing against them, and they seemed like nice people, so he went over to them.

"Hey, Gabe, what's up?" said Jacob. "You look totally stressed."

"I've had a bad night," Gabe answered.

Violence at home may pressure a child to try to escape through marijuana.

*34*　　"Hi, Gabe. Wanna cool down?" Sarah asked, and held up a metal pipe that smelled of weed.

Gabe had never smoked before. He'd never had the time to just sit around and be stoned. But he had a few hours to kill, and he needed something to calm down.

"Sure, I'll have some," Gabe said. Soon, the whole group was high as a kite, and they sat in a circle on the ground.

Gabe thought he was going insane. He had never been so frightened in his life. Every sound was his father coming to get him. Every movement was his father coming out from behind a tree. He was even more upset and nervous than when he'd left the house, and couldn't sit still, he was so jumpy. He'd never been so scared. All he wanted was to come down.

Emotional or psychological pain is always hard to handle. When we begin to feel that life is nothing but hurt, we see drugs as an escape from that hurt. Drugs seem to be able to make it all go away.

However, the pain always reappears. You can't stay high all the time. And if you try, you will find yourself with more problems than when you began. You can never escape your problems. You have to deal with them or they will follow you forever. **35**

Marijuana seems like the perfect drug for when life gets too much for you. It makes you happy and giggly, it makes you so spaced you forget all your problems. Perfect. Except that that's another myth. Your problems are there even when you're high, and getting high just makes it impossible for you to deal with them. The paranoia that pot tends to cause can make your problems seem even larger than they are. The mental confusion it causes in people makes it impossible to cope. There are better ways to help yourself than through drugs. They give you another problem: your drug use. They make you weaker, both in mind and in body. You can never take care of your life if you are sleeping all the time and can't follow the plot of a half-hour sitcom.

You never have to handle your problems on your own, especially if you find that they are taking over your life, like Gabe. You can talk to your parents, if they're not the source of the problem. You can talk to your teachers and counselors. You can call a hotline. There is help out there that will solve your problems, not just hide them for a night.

### 36 *Acceptance with Friends*

Music blasted across the room. The lights were low. The air smelled of pizza and potato chips. Yep, this was a great party all right. Carla looked at her friend Maria and smiled. "I'm sure glad you brought me. This looks like fun."

"You bet." Maria pointed toward the back of the room. "Look who's here."

Carla saw Juan sitting with Ricardo on the sofa. She waved and started toward

Sometimes it's hard to resist peer pressure to try marijuana.

them. She was hoping Juan would introduce her to Ricardo. He was the best-looking junior at South High. She had been wanting to meet him since school started.

Suddenly she stopped and stared. They were passing a joint. She didn't want to have to take a hit. The stuff always made her sick and sleepy. But no way was she going to miss out on this party. What was she going to do? She wanted to meet Ricardo.

Maria gave her a shove. "Come on, chicken. Get going. Somebody else will take the spot next to them if we don't hurry."

"Maybe we should wait a while. I can meet him later.

"No, you don't." Maria grabbed her hand and pulled her toward the couch. "You begged me to bring you here tonight. I didn't want to come because I knew what this crowd was like. You're going over there if I have to drag you."

"I'm sorry about this," Carla said. "I didn't know Ricardo smoked too."

"What did you think he did? He hangs around with Juan all the time. You know Juan smokes dope."

38 Carla didn't know what to say. She wanted to meet Ricardo, but now . . .

"What if they want me to take a hit? I can't tell them no."

"Don't say no. Just take it and drag on it lightly. They don't have to know you don't like the stuff."

"I guess." Carla shrugged, but deep inside she wished she could turn around and go home. Her cousins were there. They were lots of fun, and she never had to worry about drugs with them.

There is no rule that says you have to smoke dope to be a good friend. For all Carla knows, Ricardo may be wishing he wasn't with friends who smoked either. Sometimes we think that because others are doing something, we should too. Everyone else may be doing it because they think it is the thing to do, not because they really want to.

Imagine your best friends. Would you try to talk them into jumping off a twenty-story building? Would you send them into someone's yard if there was a mean dog growling? No. You care about your friends and want them to be safe and happy. If that is true, what kind of a friend are you if you talk someone into taking drugs? What kind of people are your friends if they try to talk you into taking drugs?

Consider also that sometimes friends want you to try something they have done because inside they know it is wrong. If they can get you to do it, maybe it won't be so bad. If they say, "Well, everyone is smoking pot. It won't hurt me," you might try to trick yourself into believing it. That is why so many of your friends want you to try drugs with them. Not because they really think it's so hot. Not because they want to hurt you. But because if they can get everyone to do it, it won't seem like such a bad thing to do.

If you are trying to quit the habit, it is easier to stay clean if you hang around with people who do not use drugs. Perhaps you don't know anyone who does not use them. That will make trying to quit tough.

There are places where you can go to meet other people. Schools have after-school activities where you can meet new friends. Large cities have community rap centers where teens can meet with other teens to talk. Religious orders have teen programs and offer many interesting activities.

Teens with positive outlooks don't need drugs to have a ball.

## *Self-Esteem*

Kerby sat on the steps of the county building trying to build up the nerve to go inside. The application for the summer job at the recreation center was neatly folded in his pocket. He really wanted that job.

Footsteps sounded behind him. He looked around to see Joe coming out of the building. Oh no! Had Joe been applying for the job? He would be much better for the position than Kerby would.

"What's up?" Kerby asked.

"I went in to sign up for summer school." Joe frowned. "My folks are making me go."

Kerby couldn't help the sigh of relief. "Tough break," he said.

Joe shook his head. "Yeah. You have to go too?"

"No. I'm applying for the job at the rec center."

"Lucky you." Joe studied Kerby. "You don't look so happy about it."

"I hate going in there and applying for the job," Kerby admitted.

"Man, I know what you mean." Joe slapped Kerby on the shoulder. "Come with me. I got something that will help."

**42**    Kerby looked at the joint Joe slid out of his pocket. A hit or two would make him feel on top of the world.

Joe pointed toward the park across the street. "We can go over there and get high. Then you'll ace that interview."

Kerby thought about it for a few minutes. He'd been high before and it always made him feel good about himself. That's what he needed for the interview. Then he remembered how his words slurred and how red his eyes would get.

"No, I better not have any now. If they think I'm taking drugs, they'll never hire me."

"Okay. It's your funeral." Joe shrugged.

Kerby wished his friend hadn't used that terminology. He watched him leave, tempted to call him back to share the joint after all.

It takes more than pot to make you feel good about yourself. Drugs can give you a false sense of esteem because they deaden your senses. When you are high you can pretend to be someone you're not.

You usually end up looking more foolish than poised. You think you are acting normal. But most people who are sober can tell when someone has been taking

Poor work in school starts with a poor attitude about yourself.

**44** marijuana. It has a tangy odor for one thing. For another, as Kerby mentioned, it makes your eyes red.

If Kerby had smoked the pot he probably would not have been hired for the job. Kerby was nervous about applying and that is normal. Most people hiring teens understand that.

There are other things Kerby could have done to build his confidence. Meditation, deep breathing exercises, and positive thinking help. Affirmations are very powerful tools also.

An affirmation is a positive statement you repeat to yourself over and over again until you believe it. For example, Kerby could have said over and over again: "I will be hired. I am confident. I will be hired. I am confident."

Positive thinking helps build self-esteem. Instead of focusing on your faults, try to see all of the good things about yourself. Kerby was so busy thinking about not getting the job that he was making himself nervous. A better way to handle that nervousness is to think of all the reasons he should get the job. Then when he is interviewed those will be in his mind and will show through.

## *Creativity*

Rhonda sat on the floor with her back against her bed. She carefully lit the joint and took a hit. After a couple of puffs, she handed the joint to her friend. "Have some, Caro. Then we'll play my new CD."

Caro reached across the bed and grabbed the joint from Rhonda. The smell of the pot filled the room. It was a good thing Rhonda's folks were never at home. Caro's mom would have a fit if she smelled pot in Caro's room.

As soon as they'd smoked about half of the joint, Rhonda began playing her new disc. She turned the volume up loud. Caro began swaying to the music.

Rhonda took another hit off the joint. "Doesn't this make the music sound much better?"

Caro listened and smiled. "It sure does." She stared at the bright colors on the poster that came with the CD. "Look at those colors. Aren't they wild?"

Both girls giggled and laughed as they listened to the music. Rhonda enjoyed the time together, but after an hour she had a splitting headache. She asked Caro to leave, then she dropped down on her bed and fell right asleep.

Some teens use drugs because they think it makes them more creative. You hear someone say all the time that getting "high" makes the music sound better. They also say they see colors and art with more vision. This is not actually true. The drug alters the mind so that it thinks music sounds better. It also changes vision so that colors seem brighter.

The truth is that while users think they

are making their vision more clear, they

Pot parties, popular in the 1960s, did not make people creative; they really damaged their brains.

are actually destroying the brain cells that are used to see. Memory loss is a proven side effect of marijuana use. If a user's goal is to be more creative, he or she is actually being less creative.

Marijuana also makes one groggy and sleepy when it starts wearing off. Rhonda's alertness soon wore off and all she wanted to do was sleep. That is certainly not creative behavior but is very typical of marijuana users.

**48** | *Mystic Levels*

Marny walked slowly down the basement steps. Kyle was ahead of her, but she still felt nervous about the darkness below.

"This is creepy," she whispered to Kyle.

"Don't be afraid." Kyle turned to assure her. "We have to do this in secret. No one ever comes down here."

Marny could believe that. She followed behind trying not to hear the creepy sounds from below nor to see the cobwebs up above. When they finally reached the basement, they had to walk down a long hall. The air was cold and damp, just like Marny's hands.

"We're almost there," Kyle told her.

He turned to her. "It's an uplifting trip. You feel like you are talking to God."

Shivers ran up and down her spine. Sometimes she felt so lost. If she could find out why she was here, she'd know what to do.

Kyle opened the door, and the light and warmth of the room welcomed them. A woman with long flowing hair sat in the middle of the room. Marny shivered again.

"Tell me again, Kyle. What do I have to do?"

"You drink the hashish oil and then lie down on those pillows. You'll see all kinds of colors and visions."

Marny stared at the woman, the pillows, and the room. Something told her to run from this place. Usually her feelings were on target.

"Take me home, Kyle. I've changed my mind."

Another thing that attracts teenagers to marijuana is its use in the mystic sense. Some teens and adults are searching for the meaning of life or who God is. Often they think that by altering their mind, they will get special vision to do this. That never happens. Drugs do alter the mind, but that removes a person from truth and God. It clouds and distorts thinking so that what is seen is not real.

If this is an attraction to you, there are proven ways to find answers to the reason for living. Every major religion has classes that offer answers. They also have people who are trained to help teens with these questions as well as those of everyday living. The next chapter will tell you how to find them.

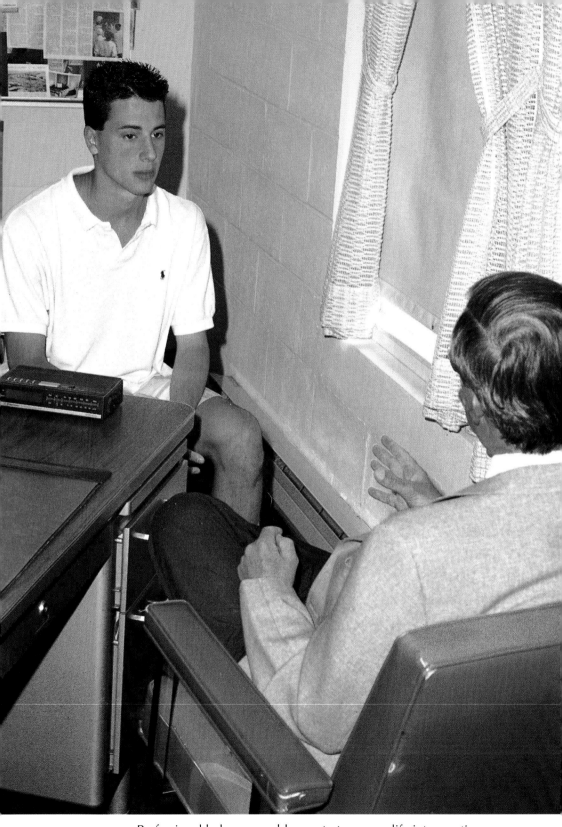

Professional help can enable you to turn your life into creative
activities.

# CHAPTER 3

# Help Is Out There

$M$arijuana is a dangerous drug. It is not physically addicting like most other drugs, but it can become a habit that is very hard to break. The important thing to realize is that any drug habit is impossible to break by yourself. A person who uses drugs, teenager or adult, needs help.

The hardest thing about asking for help is that you have to admit there is a problem. Once you do that, you can look for help. The next problem is fear. To admit a problem to yourself is one thing. But when you tell someone else, you are setting yourself up for judgment. You know you have broken a law. So it does not seem logical to go to parents, religious

**52** workers, teachers, or police for help. They seem like people who will punish you for breaking the law.

First off, look at why there is a law. The law was made because the drug is bad for you. It is like your parents' telling you not to cross the street without looking. They aren't making this rule to be mean. They don't want you to get hurt or to die.

Let's suppose a child does run into the street and is hit by a car. The child made a mistake and is in trouble. What are his parents going to do? Are they going to stand there and say, "My, my, see what happens when you don't listen?" Or are they going to gather their hurt child and say, "Here, let me help you. We'll go to the hospital where they can fix you up."

The parents are probably going to help. Parents may be hurt because their child didn't listen to their advice. But most parents love their children and want to make things right again.

It is the same in making a mistake with drugs. Try talking to your parents and see if they can help you. Maybe the parents are the problem. Many adults use marijuana. Talk to them about your concern for their health. Let them know you want them to get help. Families can go together for counseling.

If parents are unable to help, there are other places to go. Sometimes the drugs are at home and you need to find an adult friend to talk to. The Big Brother–Big Sister program offers adult friends. Teachers, school counselors, and the parks and recreation departments in your town can guide you to an adult who can be your friend. Perhaps the police officer on your beat will be someone to talk to.

Another place to look for help is in your telephone book. Look at the emergency numbers on the inside cover. Every state has an agency that provides free counseling for teenagers or adults who have a drug problem. Callers are not reported to parents or police.

This number is listed as a Crisis Service. If it lists a drug, cocaine for example, a person can call the number and get information for any drug. These agencies have lists of people who can help in any drug-related problem.

Another feature of these groups is that they will come to help if a person is having a bummer. Teenagers are often afraid to call police when a family member or

*54* friend is in trouble. They are afraid the person may be arrested. However, there is danger that the person may die. So do call the Crisis Service number. The workers are trained to help without getting the police directly involved. The sight of a uniform can frighten a person on a bummer into a heart attack. It is safer to call for help.

Another place to go for help is any major religious order near you. Jews, Catholics, and Protestants all have people who are trained to help adults and teenagers about drugs. Or they know people who can help.

Perhaps you are afraid to go to your parents or someone at the temple or church. You are afraid you will be judged. If you have admitted that you have a problem, you have already judged yourself. The rabbis, priests, and pastors of these groups are not there to judge you. They are there because they have dedicated their lives to helping others. If you are in trouble, they can help.

If by chance you get involved with a person who is more interested in judging, then back off. Find someone who will care no matter what mistakes you have

A support group can help you to realize that you are not alone
with your problems.

Talking to a trusted friend may be a good first step in getting help.

made. If you are afraid to call the clergy-person at your own temple or church, call one at another. Go with a friend to his or her religious leader.

Most temples and churches offer many services for teenagers, including help with drugs. The best part about these groups is that they will accept and care for you no matter what mistakes you have made or

what faults you have.

Most major cities have listings in the telephone book for organizations such as Jewish Family Service and Teen Challenge. Rapha is another nationally recognized health care center that offers in-hospital or outpatient care for substance abuse problems. Rapha has a 24-hour toll-free number: 1-800-227-2657.

Take a look at your life. Is your health in good order? If not, you are in danger of damaging your life. You need to decide what shape you want your body and mind to be in. You need to decide what kind of life you want to lead. After making the decision, take action. This is your life.

# Glossary
## Explaining New Words

**addiction, psychological** Compulsive feeling of need for a drug.

**affirmation** Positive statement made repeatedly until it is believed.

**biofeedback** Method of mentally controlling the automatic body functions, such as heartbeat.

**bummer** Slang term for an unpleasant reaction to a drug that is expected to provide a high.

**chemistry, body** Chemical makeup and properties of the body and its various organs.

**depressant** A sedative or something that calms.

**depression** Deep feeling of sadness; can be temporary or of long duration.

**lid**  Amount of pot sold, usually slightly less than an ounce.

**meditation**  Act of focusing the mind in order to change one's thoughts.

**mysticism**  Attempt to get in direct touch with God or truth or reality.

**narcotic**  Drug that eases pain and alters the mind.

**pain, psychological**  Mental disturbance resulting from influences outside oneself.

**roach**  Last tiny butt of a joint or reefer.

**roach clip**  Clip or bobby pin used to hold the roach.

**stoned**  Being high on pot.

**testosterone**  Hormone that develops secondary male traits, such as body hair, voice tone, and muscle distribution.

**vision**  Something unreal, seen either waking or in a dream.

**yoga**  System of physical activity designed to gain control of body or mind.

# Help List

## *Telephone Book*

### Yellow Pages
- Alcoholism, Drug Abuse, Counselors

### White Pages
- Alcoholics Anonymous, AlAnon, Narcotics Anonymous, National Council on Alcoholism, Alcoholism Counseling, Drug Abuse Services

### Government Listings
- Alcoholism Treatment, Drug Abuse, County Health Services, Child Protective Services

## *School*
- Counselors, school nurse, Drug Education and Student Services, Health Services

## *Community*
- Church
- YMCA
- YWCA

## *Write or call*

• National Association of Children of Alcoholics
31706 Pacific Coast Highway, Suite 20
South Laguna, CA 95677
(714) 499-3889

• National Council on Alcoholism
12 West 21st Street
New York, NY 10010
(212) 206-6770

• AA World Services, Inc.
P.O. Box 459
Grand Central Station
New York, NY 10163

• AlAnon Family Group Headquarters
P.O. Box 182
Madison Square Station
New York, NY 10159

• Narcotics Anonymous
World Service Office
16155 Wyandotte Street
Van Nuys, CA 91406

# For Further Reading

Gabrielle I. Edwards. *Coping with Drug Abuse.* New York: Rosen Publishing Group, 1990.

Godfrey, Martin. *Marijuana, Understanding Drugs.* New York: Franklin Watts, 1987.

Hyde, Margaret. *The Mind Drugs.* New York: McGraw-Hill, 1981.

Hyde, Margaret and Bruce. *Know About Drugs.* New York: McGraw-Hill, 1979.

Johnson, Linda Carlson. *The Value of Responsibility.* New York: Rosen Publishing Group, 1990.

McFarland, Rhoda. *Coping with Substance Abuse.* New York: Rosen Publishing Group, 1990.

Stwerthka, Eve and Albert. *Marijuana.* New York: Franklin Watts, 1979.

Wrenn, C. Gilbert, and Schwarzrock, Shirley. *The Mind Benders.* Circle Pines, MN: American Guidance Service, Inc., 1971.

# Index

**64**

### About the Author

For twenty-one years, Sandra Lee Smith has taught grades from kindergarten through college level in California and Arizona.

Active on legislative committees and in community projects, she has helped design programs to involve parents in the education process.

In response to the President's Report, *A Nation at Risk*, Ms. Smith participated in a project involving Arizona State University, Phoenix Elementary School District, and an inner-city community in Phoenix. Participants in the project developed a holistic approach to education.

### Photo Credits

Cover photo: Stuart Rabinowitz
Photos on pages 2, 25, 28, 33, 40, 50, 55, 56: Stuart Rabinowtiz; page 6: NASA; pages 10, 17, 46/74: UPI Bettmann Newsphoto; page 14: Gene Anthony/Black Star; page 19: AP/Wide World; pages 36, 43: Mary Lauzon.
Art on page 20: Sonja Kalter

**Design & Production: Blackbirch Graphics, Inc.**